GOD LOVES ME, TOO

LOU MISHLER HEATH
ILLUSTRATED BY SHEILA FORD KANE

MT. VERNON BAPTIST CHURCH LIBRARY

BROADMAN PRESS
Nashville, Tennessee

© Copyright 1979 • Broadman Press.
All rights reserved.

4242-62
ISBN: 0-8054-4262-6

Dewey Decimal Classification: C231
Subject heading: GOD/LOVE (THEOLOGY)

Printed in the United States of America.

To
Ken and Rob
Kathy and Susan
Ulka and Tim

God loves each person.
    The grown-ups and children small
And all the sizes in between —
    He dearly loves them all.

4

God made each person special:
    Each child, each dad, each mother.
And since we all do different things,
    We each can help the other.

6

If God loves us, the Bible says,
    We ought to love each other
And treat each person that we meet
    As though he is our brother.

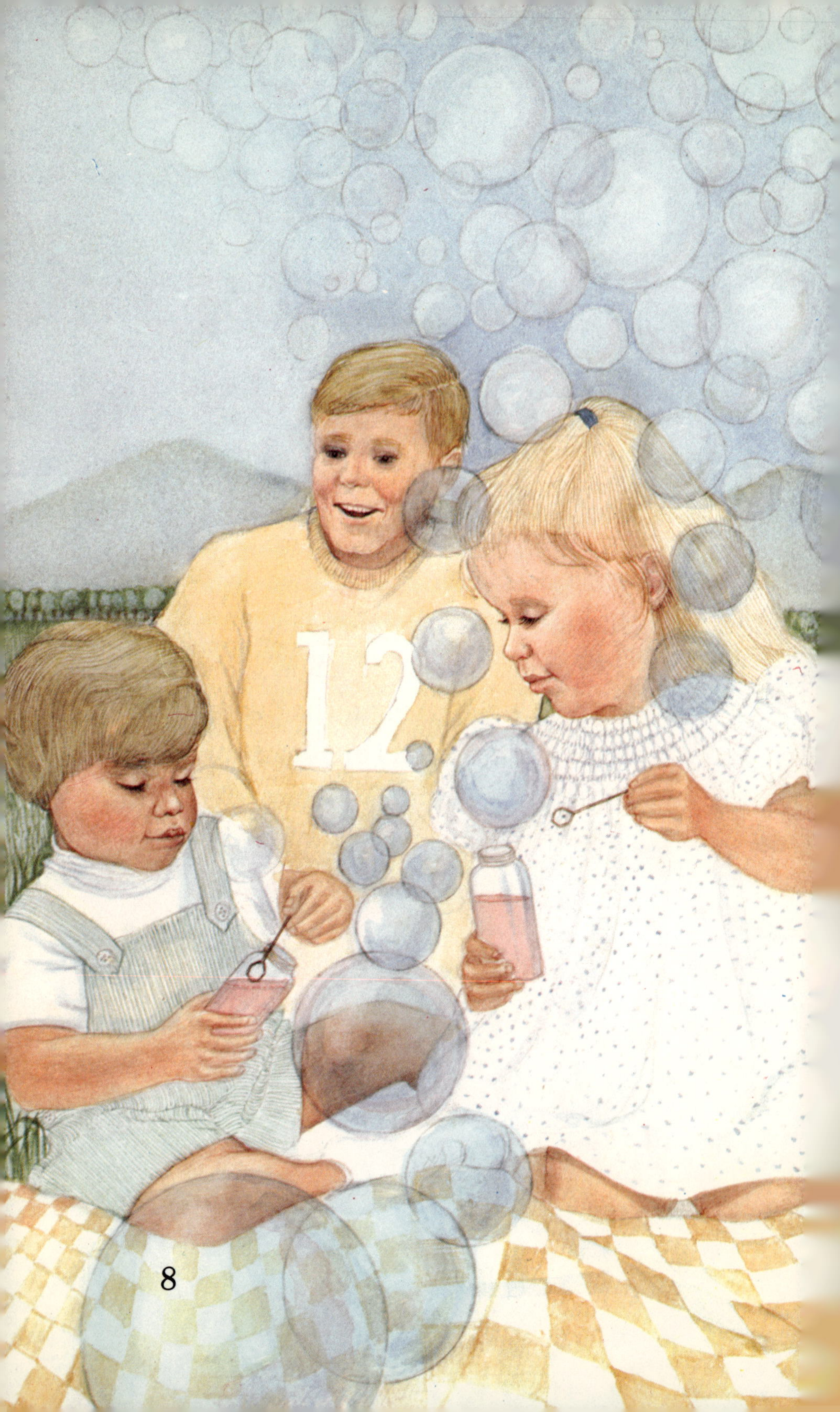
12

Jesus never chose his friends,
    By size, or age it's true.
He tried to be a friend to all,
    And that's what I will do.

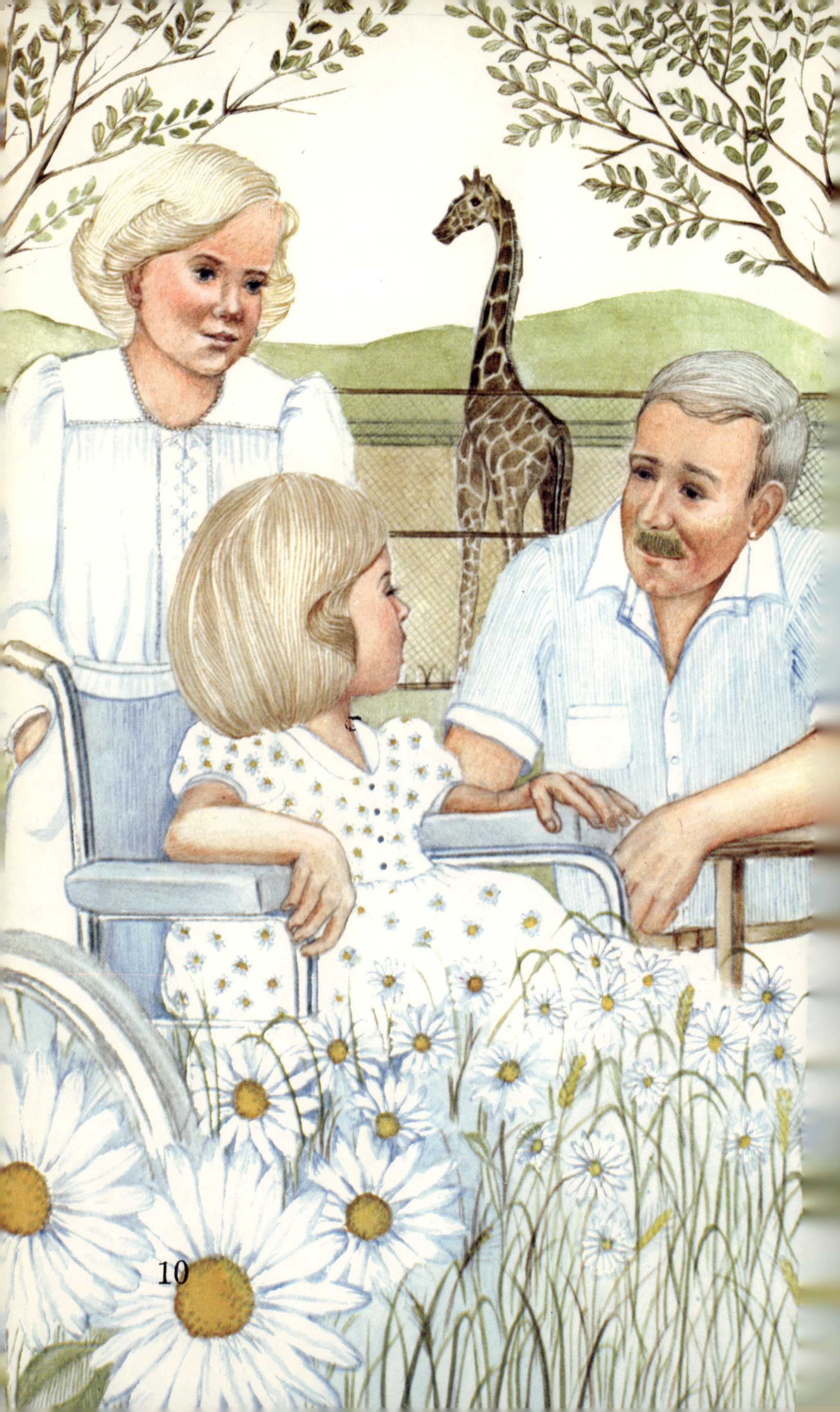

Jesus loved a blind man;
    Jesus didn't stare.
He stopped to be a helper;
    He showed his love and care.

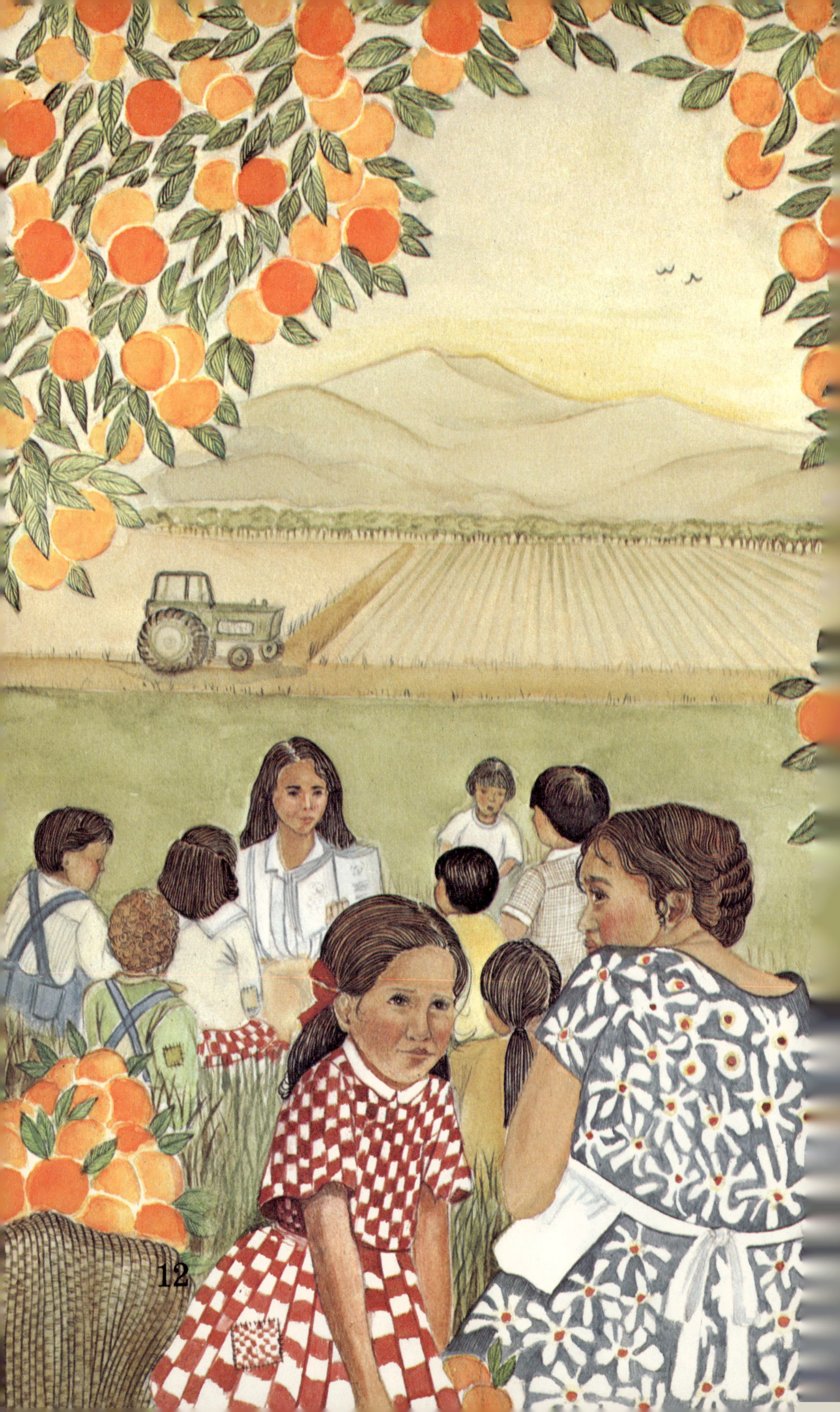

Jesus never would make fun
    Of someone poorly dressed.
He treated everyone the same,
    Just like an honored guest!

14

Jesus loved some people
    The neighbors said were bad.
And he loves me when I'm not good,
    Although it makes him sad.

16

John has a problem when he talks.
    He stutters; so does Kyle.
I know God loves them just the same;
    I'll show them with a smile.

18

Reading's hard for some of us.
    For Jodi, math is too.
Being rude by making fun
    Is not the thing to do.

20

I can't bat as well as Mike,
    Or read as fast as Paul.
If each of us just does his best,
    It shouldn't matter at all!

22

There isn't anyone all bad,
    Or anyone all good.
So each one needs to help the other
    To do the things we should.

24

Ulka's eyes and skin are brown.
Susan's eyes are blue.
Darylene has freckles on her skin
And lots of red hair too.

26

Sometimes when I see people
    Who do not look like me
I wonder when they look my way,
    If they like what they see.

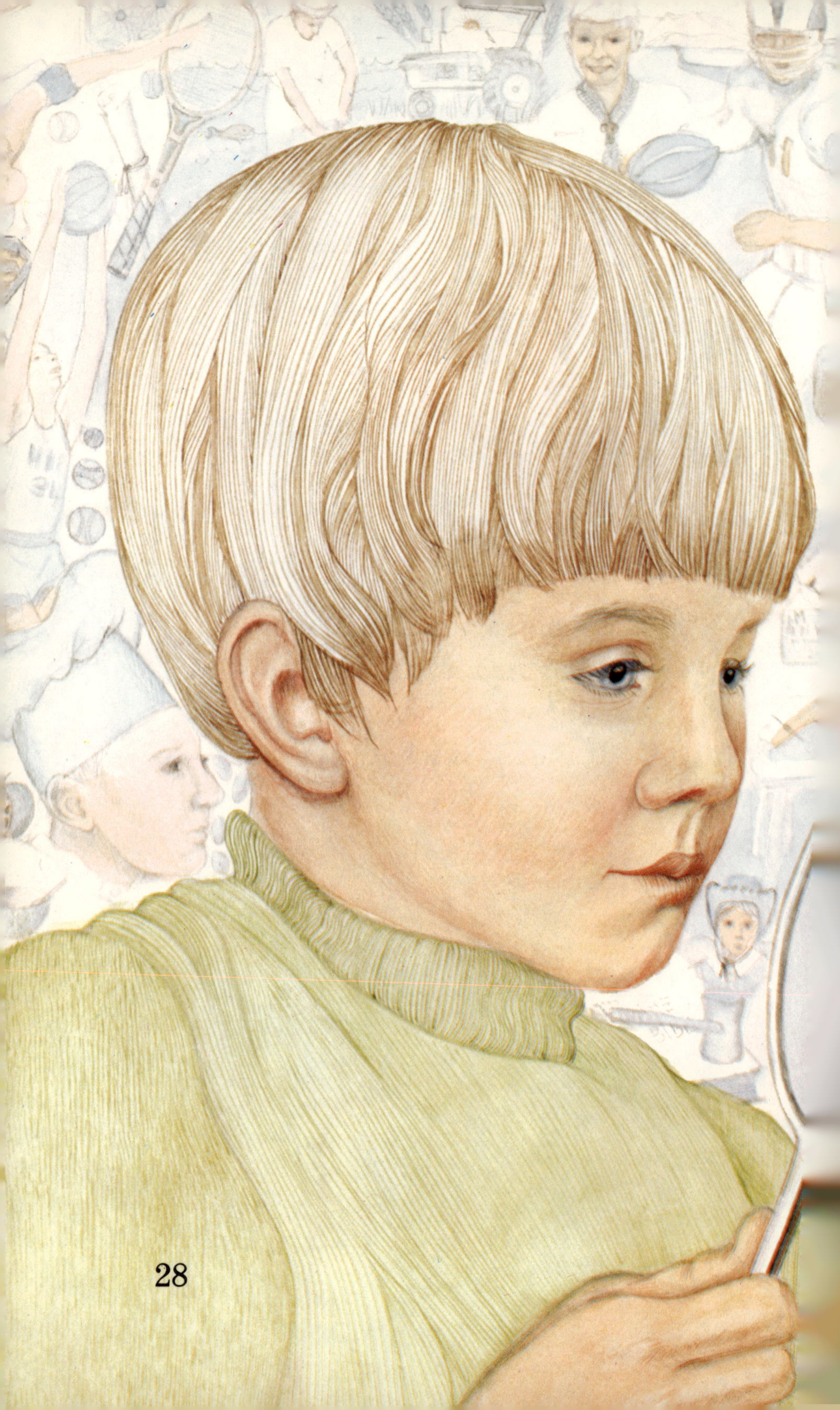

A mirror doesn't tell you much;
    It's just an outside view.
It cannot show what God has planned
    To one day make of you.

30

Look at people everywhere;
  God loves each one the same.
I'm glad he loves me as I am,
  And that he knows my name!

31

Isn't it wonderful
    That God loves you?
And though we are different,
    God loves me, too.

Date Due

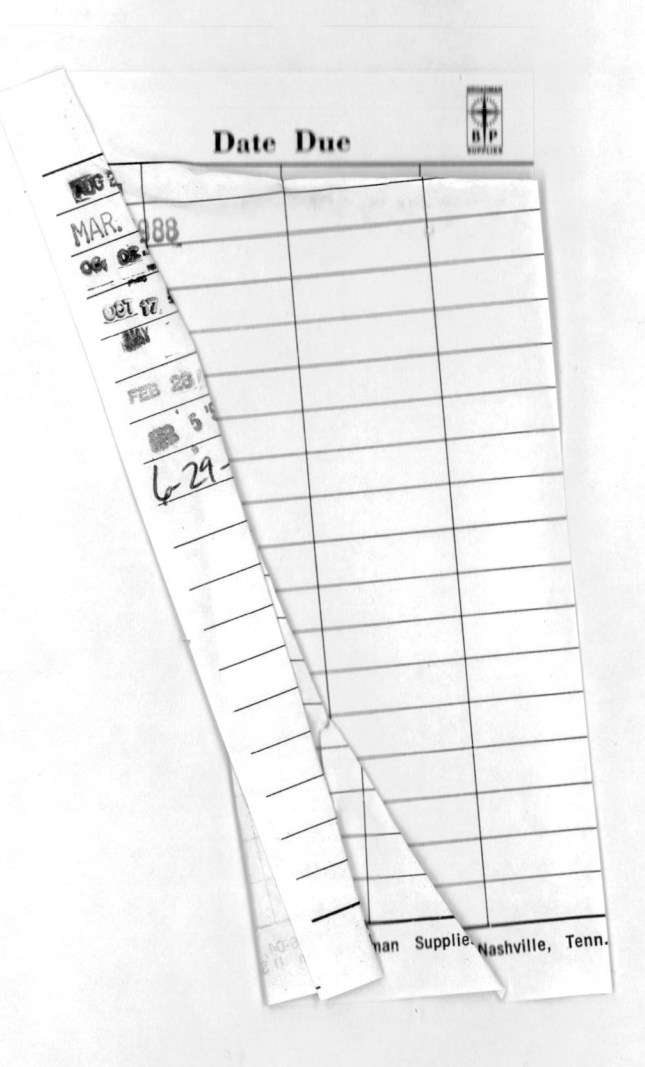

AUG		
MAR. 988		
OC 02		
OCT 17		
FEB 28		
R 5		
6-29-		

...man Supplies, Nashville, Tenn.